Mo

*Learn how to motivate and inspire
people to be happy and productive*

Kate Keenan

Pocket
Manager
Books

Published by Pocket Manager Books
1 Queen Square
Bath BA1 2HA

www.pocketmanagerbooks.com

Print ISBN 978-1-909179-53-0
eBook ISBN: 978-1-909179-66-0
Pdf ISBN: 978-1-909179-80-6

A CIP catalogue record for this book is available from the
British Library.

Previously published as The Management Guide to Motivating by
Oval Books, 1995, 1997.

Original series editor – Anne Tauté, Oval Books
Editor – Catriona Tulloch Scott
Project manager – Clare Christian, The Book Guru
Book and cover re-design – Philip Jansseune, Walker Jansseune
Image enhancement – Matt Holland, MiH Design
Author photograph – Marko Dutka, Studio Marko

*Cover: Newton's cradle– for every action there is an equal and
opposite reaction.*

Contents

This book is dedicated to
those who would like to manage better
but are too busy to begin.

To download your **FREE** Workbook
which accompanies
Motivate

please visit:

**www.pocketmanagerbooks.com/books/
motivate**

Motivate

The concept of motivation is often seen as a mystery, a commodity something akin to magic dust which you sprinkle over people and suddenly everyone is full of energy and a willingness to work productively.

In fact, the concept of motivation is remarkably simple. It has to do with how well individuals are treated and how good they feel about what they are doing. However, what you have to do to get people motivated, and then to keep them that way, is not quite so easy.

This book helps you understand the nature of motivation and gives some practical suggestions as to how to go about creating highly motivated people and then sustaining their momentum.

1 The need for motivation

Being motivated is a vital aspect in wanting to work well. It has to do with how committed people are to doing their work and achieving their goals, even if these are as basic as the wish to make more money or go home early.

Unfortunately, it is all too easy for people to lose motivation. The signs of low morale can often become the norm if nothing is done to rectify them.

Signs of low morale

Recognising that people are not motivated is not quite as straightforward as it sounds. They do not always tell you how they are feeling or admit that they are dissatisfied, but they can often show signs of not being happy with their lot. When things are going well there is usually an atmosphere of energy and interest which you can readily sense. If this is absent, it should alert you straight away.

Discontent will also be reflected in general behaviour and some of the signs to look out for are:

- Not co-operating when extra effort is needed.
- Being reluctant to volunteer to do extra things.
- Arriving late, leaving early, or taking a day off without a satisfactory explanation.
- Dragging out tea-breaks and mealtimes to get the maximum amount of time away from working.

- Missing deadlines because tasks have not been completed on time.
- Not coming up to standard.
- Complaining constantly about trivial things.
- Blaming others when things are not working well.
- Neglecting to follow instructions.

The presence of just one of these negative aspects does not necessarily mean that people are demotivated, but a combination of two or three should make warning bells ring. People's behaviour may be telling you something about the situation in which they are working or perhaps the way they are being managed.

You need to find out what could be causing this demoralisation and then to try work out what would motivate people to improve.

Negative reactions

When things are not going as well as they should be, people will often express opinions and demonstrate attitudes which suggest that they are not happy.

Here are some classic phrases which you might have heard being used to vent these feelings:

- *'It should never have happened.'* Time spent apportioning the blame for the current mess, rather than solving the problem, is counter-productive.

- *'If only they'd listened to us.'* Harping back to the past and mulling over failures only lowers morale.
- *'What a company to work for.'* Probably the most self-defeating attitude of all, because if it is such a dreadful company, why are people still working there?
- *'I'm always the last to know.'* When communication is not working properly, or is perhaps non-existent, people find it difficult to be engaged or motivated.
- *'It's all their fault.'* By blaming a nebulous group of others, people can feel that there is no need to take personal responsibility for their own actions.
- *'So what's new?'* The situation is grudgingly accepted, and there is little motivation to do anything about it.
- *'Who cares anyway?'* People are less likely to take personal responsibility if they produce poor work.
- *'I might have known that would happen.'* There is no expectation that work should be of a high standard.
- *'Nobody ever tells me anything.'* People feel helpless and not in control of what they are doing.

All these responses point to the presence of underlying negative attitudes which are all too readily communicated to others. The few who are themselves demoralised and disengaged can unwittingly demotivate a large number of people incredibly easily. Once people are demotivated, it is so much more difficult to restore morale and improve the willingness to want to work well.

Poor performance

It is all too easy to attribute poor performance to a lack of motivation. In reality there are a number of reasons why this may occur, none of which may have anything to do with individual motivation. Some of the factors which prevent good performance might be:

- **Insufficient training** If there have been substantial changes to the job, people may not be as competent as they were and therefore more reluctant to make an effort. Or it may be that relevant training has not been provided from the start.
- **Incompetence** If people are not competent in their jobs, you may get the impression that they are just lazy. Few people are prepared to admit that they lack knowledge or ability; they will usually offer excuses as to why the work cannot be or has not been done.
- **Weak discipline** If disciplinary procedures are rarely used to the limit, this can cause people to push boundaries, leading to a cynical attitude to work.
- **Low standards** If the performance standards of a task have not been clearly defined, it could seem to the person doing the work that *'Whatever I do, it's wrong.'*
- **Poor management** If people have been badly managed in the past, they may have little respect for control of any sort. They will probably what they are told to do, but their responses may be less than enthusiastic.

- **Personal problems** If a substantial change in an individual's attitude occurs, it may signal that domestic difficulties have become insurmountable.

Being aware of some of the various causes which could underpin poor performance is the first step in finding a solution.

The key motivators

Understanding what motivates individuals can be puzzling. It is often a mistake to think that people are motivated by the more obvious material objectives and you may be underestimating their aspirations.

The most common and mistaken beliefs about what motivates people are:

- They just work for the money.
- They need the security of the job.
- They like being with other people and enjoy the support of the group.

In fact, these are elements which tend to prevent people from feeling too dissatisfied with their lot, but they do not actually encourage them to work any harder or put in the extra effort.

What seems to motivate people has to do with the results of their own efforts and the feeling that they are contributing to the overall success of the enterprise. People tend to be more motivated to work harder when they can:

- **Achieve things** When people are able to achieve things and see the tangible results of their personal efforts, they usually find the work more motivating.
- **Do things their own way** When people are allowed the freedom to do things in an individual way which suits them, this inspires them to achieving great things.
- **Take on responsibility** When people have the chance to be responsible for what needs to be done, they are more likely to make sure things happen.

All these elements are based on the idea that people are motivated by the opportunity to obtain personal achievement and recognition, which are key motivators.

Tackle demotivation

Demotivation is insidious. It is like having toothache: not life-threatening, but debilitating. Being able to spot that people are not happy in what they are doing is an essential requirement if you are to be able to motivate them.

Addressing the reasons for poor performance and working to eliminate negative attitudes, as well as understanding individual needs, are all key components in the process of motivating people to want to work better.

Questions to ask yourself

Think about the people with whom you work and ask
yourself the following questions:

- Do people seem somewhat unwilling to make an extra
  effort?

- Do they constantly moan about trivialities?

- Are they rarely there when I need them?

- Do they always seem to blame others, possibly me,
  when things go wrong?

- Have there been any substantial changes to the work
  environment or the business itself?

- Are people finding their work more difficult than
  previously?

- Do I tend to simplify the factors which are likely to
  motivate people?

If you have answered 'Yes' to some or all of these questions,
you may need to give some thought to how motivated
people are.

You will be doing better if...

- You can recognise when people seem not to be as motivated as you would like them to be.

- You can identify some of the factors that might be causing demotivation.

- You can diagnose the possible reasons for this.

- You are sensitive to where there are negative reactions, along with an atmosphere which indicates that all might not be well.

- You are able to distinguish where poor performance may be due to factors other than lack of motivation.

- You realise that it is easy to misunderstand the elements that motivate people.

2 Understand basic needs

To understand what motivates people, you need to appreciate that people have a number of basic needs that drive them to thrive and prosper. These take the form of driving forces which everyone is motivated to satisfy.

The driving forces

There are three fundamental areas in life that people require to satisfy. These can be viewed as three levels, which together form a hierarchy of needs.

Level 1: Basic requirements

The basic needs – food, water and warmth – require to be satisfied if you are to survive. These needs cannot be ignored nor wished away. If you were living in the wild you would need to hunt and fish to feed yourself. In a mostly urban society this need is converted to earning a living to supply the necessities. In most societies, money is the medium through which these needs are satisfied, as it provides the wherewithal to assuage hunger, thirst and cold.

But money alone can never provide total motivation. Salary or wages act as motivators only in that they provide the answer to the question, *'Why go to work?'* Many people think that the more you pay people, the more they will be motivated. However, money can only really motivate people to get out of bed and go to work. Provided the payment hovers around the accepted level for the job, money itself tends to have very little effect in getting people to produce sustained extra effort.

To increase the amount of money paid for the job will not necessarily make them want to work better. For example, a pay rise of £50 a week will soon be absorbed into normal living costs and people will wonder how on earth they managed previously.

Once the basic drives are satisfied through earning enough money to provide what is essential, it is the higher level needs that begin to make themselves felt.

Level 2: Social status

People need to feel that they belong. They work to acquire a definite place in their society. Social needs differ within different cultures and people work to achieve these needs in accordance with the customs of their own societies.

If you live in a tribal village in Outer Mongolia, the acquisition of another yak may give you added social status. In most Western societies, the equivalent would be a large house or an expensive car. For example, having a luxury sports car might be one way of satisfying the need for self-esteem since it can indicate an individual's position in society or, if it's a company car, their perceived value to the business. For others, this might be achieved by a more prestigious job title or a bigger office.

Expressions of social status are important to people and are powerful motivators once the physiological drives are satisfied. People will also work better for incentives, such as a prize holiday for being top salesman. This is not just because the prize in itself is enjoyable, but because winning it clearly distinguishes a person's achievement when compared with that of his or her colleagues. For some, this makes the effort worthwhile.

Level 3: Personal ambitions

Neither basic requirements nor social status tell the whole story, for neither is an entirely sufficient explanation. The third and most powerful driving force is to satisfy personal ambitions.

People want to develop themselves and do better at their chosen occupation. This means setting individual objectives which can enhance personal development, and working towards their achievement.

Often there is no apparent rhyme nor reason why someone seeks a certain goal, or is determined to achieve a specific objective. These individual ambitions are usually related to something that has captured the imagination or in which a talent has been demonstrated. People tend to work hard at things they are good at.

The desire to achieve personal aspirations is a powerful motivator and is a continuous process. It never ceases because as soon as one ambition is achieved, another usually presents itself. The need for people to realise ambition is a far more compelling force than is often recognised.

Motivating effects

The three primary needs, basic requirements, social status and personal ambitions, can all be operating at the same time.

The higher needs are extremely influential, but they are meaningless if the other lower needs are not reasonably satisfied. If, for example, the need to achieve personal ambition is frustrated, an increase in the other levels of need may well take place.

So it is useful to recognise the following:

- Once a basic need has been satisfied, there will be an instant desire to satisfy those needs which have yet to be satisfied.
- The less a particular need is satisfied, the more important it becomes.
- The less a higher level need is satisfied, the greater the importance a lower level one will tend to assume.

If people cannot get what they want, such as the ability to develop their skills, they will tend to demand more of what they can get. Hence, the demand for more money may be hiding a desire for a more challenging job, or a hankering for perks may be masking a need to be appreciated by others.

Motivation and basic needs

There are basic drives which everyone seeks to satisfy. Together these form the mainspring of human behaviour and its motivation.

Unless lower order needs are satisfied, motivation is impossible. The fulfilment of these needs takes away dissatisfaction and prevents people feeling disgruntled about their lot. It does not necessarily motivate people to do better and improve their productivity.

Having an understanding of people's basic needs is essential, for without this knowledge you cannot start to appreciate how you can go about motivating others.

Questions to ask yourself

Think about the basic needs people have, and ask yourself the following questions:

- Do I appreciate that there are driving forces which everyone requires to satisfy?

- Do I understand the part that money can play in satisfying these drives?

- Do I recognise the social needs which people desire to be fulfilled?

- Do I understand the individual nature of personal ambition?

- Do I realise that the satisfaction of basic requirements does not necessarily motivate people to improve their performance?

- Do I understand that if people ask for more to satisfy a lower level need, this could be because their higher level needs are not being met?

You will be doing better if…

- You recognise the various levels of driving forces which people require to satisfy.

- You realise the part that money can play in satisfying these drives.

- You appreciate that the less a basic need is satisfied, the more importance it assumes.

- You understand that satisfying basic requirements does not necessarily motivate people to improve their performance.

3 Design the work

Understanding the needs that people require to be satisfied is one thing. Understanding what motivates people to work well is another thing altogether. To get people to want to work to their fullest potential means ensuring that the right conditions are created and that what they are doing is a source of satisfaction to them, something they think is worth doing.

To do this you need to understand how work can be designed to provide people with the best possible level of job satisfaction.

The need to do something worthwhile

People who lack motivation are often viewed as being lazy, with the assumption that lazy people usually lack motivation. This is not true. More often than not, the cause of dissatisfaction is not the job itself, but the conditions in which it is done. For example, a person will read a novel in one sitting, but will get bored after twenty minutes when studying a textbook. Or, someone may find pressing buttons repetitive and tedious when working on an assembly line, but will spend hours performing precisely the same action on a play station.

It is not the activity which produces demotivation or boredom, it is the content or the situation in which it is being carried out. If people do not achieve satisfying outcomes from their activities, they tend to perceive them as tedious and not worth doing.

Create the right conditions

When people are asked to indicate what they like and dislike about their work, the aspects they say they like are usually significantly different from the ones they dislike. They are rarely the direct opposite of each other. For example, people usually feel good when they:

- Are skilled at doing the work itself.
- Can achieve a high standard.
- Have their efforts recognised.

These are underlying or intrinsic aspects which relate directly to making a specific effort and are under the personal control of the individual. Whereas, the sorts of things people feel dissatisfied about are:

- Company policy and methods.
- Red tape and bureaucracy.
- Inadequate working conditions.

These are external or extrinsic features of work, things over which most people have little control. What is more, if the causes of dissatisfaction are eliminated, motivation to do better does not automatically ensue.

For people to be motivated, you need to ensure they are given the opportunities to carry out activities which they find rewarding, and to protect them from those things that may interfere with the completion of their tasks.

Provide satisfaction

For people to give their best to their work, they need to have pride in it and to gain pleasure from it. In order for work to provide satisfaction, people need to:

- **Perceive the work as meaningful** If the job appears to be important and interesting, people are more likely to feel motivated.
- **Be made accountable for the results of the work** If people view the quality of work they do as dependant upon their personal effort rather than upon outside factors, they will tend to feel more proud of the outcomes. They will be far more concerned to ensure that the work is up to standard.
- **Be given feedback on performance** If people regularly find out how well they are performing, they will feel appreciated and be stimulated to do better.

It is worth looking at these three factors, work content, accountability and feedback, in more detail in order to identify what you need to do to provide as many of these 'job satisfying' conditions as possible.

Meaningful work

For people to feel that what they are doing is meaningful, and therefore is worthwhile doing, the work to be done needs to be of a high quality and contain varied components. People need to:

- **Have different things to do** Doing the same, limited task all the time can be soul-destroying. People are likely to consider that what they are doing is worthwhile if they carry out a variety of activities which develop and demonstrate their abilities.
- **Complete the whole task** Doing it all rather than only a small part, or seeing something through to the finish and being able to say, *'I did that'* or *'I made this'* is satisfying. Being shown the end product may also help to engender this feeling.
- **Produce or do something benefical** Doing something which is of assistance to others or making something useful enables people to feel that they are helpful and making a contribution.

To analyse the work that people do you need to consult them. This helps you to find out if their work is providing them with the variety and range of activities which bring them satisfaction. It gives them the chance to let you know if reorganising their tasks might provide them with the opportunity to produce a better quality of work.

Accountability and autonomy

For people to feel good about their work, the right level of autonomy needs to be provided and fostered, along with the right level of accountability. This means you need to:

- **Allow freedom** Instead of giving orders, offer people the discretion to carry out and schedule their tasks. This encourages them to devise their own methods and makes them readier and happier to take responsibility.
- **Give power** Instead of making all the decisions, make people accountable for the results of their work. This allows them to take a personal pride in whatever they are doing.

It is important that you give people the opportunity to take on responsibility. By becoming more involved in their work they will be far more willing to take responsibility and be held to account for results.

Therefore you need to establish which individuals would like to be made more responsible in one way or another. This often produces surprising results. For instance, someone who works a strict 9-5 day and who is thought to be uninterested in the work, is discovered to be thoroughly frustrated by the lack of responsibility and is yearning to take on more; and when given it, works round the clock.

Shouldering desired responsibility is a great motivator;

so is taking on extra responsibilities, provided you make it clear to people that this is a way they can develop themselves, and that you take an obvious interest in their progress.

The more you can provide the conditions for individuals to feel that they manage their own destiny at work, the more involved they will feel, and the more prepared they will be to make the extra effort required to achieve a successful outcome.

Constructive feedback

For people to perform better they need to receive feedback about how they are doing. Before you can do this, you need to:

- **Agree clear and attainable standards** This provides people with a yardstick against which they can measure their performance, allowing them to get feedback for themselves from their own experience.
- **Have regular reviews** This allows people to let you know about their problems and discuss methods of improving performance.

Telling people how well they are performing, and indicating in a sympathetic and constructive way where improvement might be made, provides them with the motive to do better. To do this, you should:

- See them on a regular basis.
- Discuss their performance and agree where they are doing well as well as where they would be able to do better.
- Find out what else they would like to do, and what they would like someone else to do.
- Agree the methods and facilities for doing so.
- Follow up the results of those ideas and confirm that any improvements made are having the desired effect.
- Be constructive when critical.
- Praise when performance is good.

In this way, people learn about the areas where they need to do better, and are also encouraged and motivated to carry on good work where they are already doing well.

Worthwhile work

It is important that you do all you can to ensure that the right conditions are present for motivating people to work well. For work to give satisfaction, people must feel that they are doing something worthwhile. They also need to know the importance of their work and to be allowed to complete as much of the whole task as possible.

By allowing people to take responsibility, they can take control of what they are doing, and so feel that they are making a positive contribution. Knowing how well they are achieving their work provides them with the encouragement to keep doing what they are doing well, and directs their attention to those tasks they could do better.

The more meaningful you can make the work, the more interest people will take in what they are doing. The more freedom you allow people, the more they will be prepared to be accountable for the results. The more you let them know how well they are functioning, the more personal satisfaction they will get from doing the job itself.

Together, all these conditions create a solid foundation for people to want to work better and to put in that extra effort.

Questions to ask yourself

Think about the work that people are required to carry out and answer the following questions:

- Are people given the opportunity to do those things which come under their personal control?

- Do they perceive their work as worthwhile?

- Do they have a variety of tasks to do?

- Are they able to see a task through to completion, or at least see the end product?

- Are they being offered responsibility?

- Are they being provided with feedback on how well they are doing?

- Are constructive suggestions offered for those areas that need improving?

- Is everything being done to ensure that people have the best possible conditions to achieve satisfaction from their work?

You will be doing better if...

- You know what people enjoy about their work and discuss how things can be improved in areas they find frustrating.

- You ensure that they know the significance of what they are doing in the grand order of things.

- You let them do as much as is feasibly possible of the whole task.

- You enable them to take on as much responsibility as they want to.

- You provide regular and constructive feedback on performance.

4 Inspire performance

Motivating people to want to achieve results means inspiring them to want to do well. To encourage people to do better at their work, and be more creative, you have to set up a suitable climate for them to want to make that extra effort.

The amount of effort you put in to creating the right working environment is directly related to the level of performance you inspire.

Ensure competence

An underlying pre-condition to inspiring performance is making sure that people are able to carry out their activities competently. Competent people are far more confident in their abilities and so are more motivated.

Any changes to work patterns or any additional responsibilities may alter an individual's level of competence. And the requirement to develop new skills may mean that some people are no longer quite as capable as they once were.

Some of the signs to notice which indicate a reduced level of competence are frustration, loss of confidence and reluctance to accept responsibility. If this is the case, you need to identify the areas where people are not performing to standard, or are unsure of their ability, and help them acquire the appropriate skills.

There are several simple ways of doing this:

- **External formal training experience** This will provide both theory and practice, such as courses for a day or a week, etc.
- **In-house training** This will enable practical, specific skills to be learned. For example, sitting at 'Nellie's elbow', provided that 'Nellie' possesses the appropriate expertise and a constructive attitude.
- **One-to-one coaching** This will provide expertise that is tailored to specific needs. As this can be precisely focused to individual needs, coaching can be a cost effective way of developing competence.

These methods to improve performance can also contribute to a recognised qualification, thus providing another incentive to do well. Make sure that after people have undergone training you review their progress and give praise for work well done. By helping people to perform better you show that you are interested in them, which in itself is motivating.

Accommodate individual needs

Tailoring work to meet individual needs is a clear way of showing people that they are valued. By taking time to think about what people need, you will be able to work out how you might be able to accommodate these needs within the work that you require them to do. For instance, you could:

- **Enable people to work flexi-time or core time** For example, a 24-hour week or 10.00-4.00 each day, or have the option to work part-time when it suits them better. Identify the various options available to individuals. If two people are to share a job, ensure that duties are agreed and hand-overs are worked out.
- **Allow time during working hours for important personal appointments** For example, visits to the dentist, doctor, parent/teacher meetings, etc. Agree times and dates of such visits so that you are able to arrange for jobs to be covered as required.
- **Encourage opportunities to socialise** For example, arranging a social evening after work or negotiating a discount for the membership of a local gymnasium; Better still, obtain suggestions from people themselves and encourage those who are most interested to organise the activities.

Allowing individuals to work in a way which suits them means they feel they are appreciated in their work and therefore they are likely to work harder.

Relieving people of unnecessary stress and worry in their personal lives should enable them to give their full attention to their work.

Encouraging them to get to know each other better forms more productive working relationships, resulting in a higher level of output.

Provide incentives

The provision of incentives is based on the premise that people will increase their efforts when they are given a specific reward or encouragement for good performance. Incentives tend to work best when the following conditions apply:

- The reward on offer is perceived as worth having and worth making an extra effort for.
- The additional performance can be measured objectively and directly accredited to individual achievement.
- The increased level of performance does not become the new minimum standard.

If the first two conditions do not apply, receiving an incentive will be considered to be a nice extra, but will not necessarily cause people to want to perform more productively.

If the third condition is violated, the incentive will cease to be regarded as a motivator. For example, if an extra effort is required for a rush job, everyone may be quite happy to give up half an hour at lunchtime in return for half a day off when the job is completed. But if people subsequently find that from then on they are expected to take less time for lunch, this would cause them to become disillusioned and less willing to make an extra effort next time.

If incentives are to produce the results you desire, you need to work out what sort of reward would be effective in motivating people. So discuss this with the people concerned and make sure the promised reward is forthcoming when the target is achieved.

Praise positively

People value being praised when they have performed well. If they have put in an extra effort, receiving praise for a job well done makes them feel it was all worthwhile. You need to:

- Recognise the situation in which people should be praised instead of letting good work slide by without notice or without calling attention to it.
- Make time to say, *'Well done'* rather than throwing a cursory *'Thanks'* over your shoulder on your way out.
- Give unconditional praise for work well done.

It is important to give unconditional praise, *'That is/was brilliant',* because if you praise and criticise in the same breath, for example, *'You did that very well, but...',* you will get the reputation for being a 'but' person, someone who is never pleased.

Many people mistakenly believe that they can use praise for the bit which is right to sweeten the criticism of the unsatisfactory bit. But those receiving criticism will only remember the criticism and never the praise. This tends to have the effect of demotivating them instead of motivating them and reduced levels of performance will almost certainly result.

However, when there is a justifiable need to criticise, by all means do so. Then, when the task is completed to the right standard, wholeheartedly give the praise that is due. The point is to make sure you do these things on entirely separate occasions, even if they are only ten minutes apart. This way your praise will achieve its positive and motivating effect.

Stimulate motivation

To stimulate motivation you need to make sure people are competent, and that you accommodate their individual needs where possible, provide appropriate incentives and, above all, praise them wholeheartedly. This way, you inspire people to want to perform well.

Questions to ask yourself

Think about how you ensure that people are motivated and answer the following questions:

- Are people fully competent in the tasks they are required to perform?

- Have conditions changed so that those who are usually competent are suddenly demonstrating signs of incompetence and frustration?

- Have I explored various training options for restoring and/or improving levels of performance?

- Have I looked at the possibility of tailoring the work to fit individual needs?

- Do people consider the incentives offered are worth working for?

- Do I praise people unreservedly when they have achieved good work?

- Do I make sure that I do not mingle criticism with praise?

- Do I praise people enough?

You will be doing better if…

- You encourage people to make their own decisions.

- You make sure that people are capable of carrying out their tasks.

- You understand the conditions under which incentives could be productive.

- You are prepared to adapt the work to fit in with individual needs wherever possible.

- You provide extra facilities which will assist people in managing their outside responsibilities better.

- You give constructive and detailed criticism.

- You make sure that any criticism of performance is given on an entirely separate occasion from any praise given for performance.

- You are confident that you praise people for their efforts.

5 Maintain motivation

Once people are performing in a highly-motivated way, it is important to help them maintain their momentum. This is done by keeping a watchful eye on standards and morale. If you do not notice when effort falls below standard, people will think you do not care. And if you do not sense when morale is low, output could rapidly deteriorate. Both these conditions are essential to maintaining high levels of motivation.

There are several practical ways of keeping morale at a high level.

Keep people informed

The more people know about what is happening, the more confident they are about their work and this has a positive impact on maintaining morale.

Keeping people informed does not mean telling them about plans which are confidential or disclosing anything that is commercially sensitive.

It simply means ensuring that the information people are given is as correct and as up-do-date as that which is available to you. You need to:

- Keep yourself informed about what is going on.
- Let people know as soon as you do.
- Explain how the information could affect them.

A lack of knowledge usually lowers morale and, therefore, motivation, and usually leads to negative speculation. So make sure that you pass on information accurately and immediately, preferably in person.

Sustain performance

Once motivation is present, like the oil that keeps the cogs turning in a machine, you need to ensure that standards of performance are constantly topped up.

There are three basic ways of doing this:

- A regular maintenance.
- A major overhaul when required.
- A review at agreed intervals.

For these activities to be effective, you need to carry them out in a positive and encouraging way.

Day-to-day maintenance

No matter how motivated people are, they need to know that their efforts are being appreciated. They will also value being advised when they could do something better before it becomes a major problem. It is demoralising to be told that something has not been done properly for some time when calling attention to it earlier would have made all the difference.

This means you need to keep a watchful eye on what is

going on to ensure that things are running smoothly and that you make minor adjustments when they are required.

Some key things you can do are to:

● **Show concern** Focus on the people themselves and not just
their work.
● **Encourage discussion** Talk about how their work is going and give practical advice when appropriate.
● **Point out where minor improvements need to made** Discuss what can be done and how to do it.

People like to feel that what they are doing is being noticed and that they are playing a valuable part in ensuring the success of the enterprise.

Major overhaul

Sometimes, no matter how hard you work to motivate people and encourage them to achieve what is required, their performance still remains below standard and it is obvious that they are not motivated.

It is easy to assume that this is due to reluctance or a poor attitude. The temptation is to express exasperation or annoyance, *'How many times have I told her...?'* *'He never does what he's supposed to do,'* without realising the demotivating effect this can have on other people who are within earshot.

Rather than reacting antagonistically or showing irritation, it's important that you control your feelings and plan a course of action. You need to:

- **Identify the precise area or area where a gap has occurred** Indicate where existing performance and the expected standards of performance are not in sync.
- **Fix a time** See the individual privately and ensure that no-one else can overhear.
- **Ask questions** Find out why performance is below standard.
- **Agree a course of action** Get commitment for improvement.

You must also make it clear that you want this person to succeed and that you will be giving him or her as much help and encouragement as you can.

Performance review

Day-to-day maintenance and the occasional overhaul keep things ticking over but do not necessarily show that things are on target.

To check this, you need to carry out a periodic performance review, rather like the MOT for cars ensures that they are roadworthy. This helps people to see how they are progressing and gives them the impetus to carry on the good work. The topics to discuss are:

- **Past performance** What a person feels he/she has achieved and what could have been done better.
- **Future activities or plans** What is likely to happen and what part the person would play in this.
- **Objectives** What additional responsibilities the person might take on.

A periodic review provides people with an overall sense of direction, a feeling that they know where they are going. It also provides a reference point to return to if things become fraught.

All these ways of reviewing performance are key elements in helping to maintain motivation by keeping people on track and enabling them to focus clearly on what they are trying to achieve.

Encourage enthusiasm

Individual personalities can influence levels of morale. How this is controlled or harnessed is important if confidence is to be maintained.

Occasionally you may find there is someone in the team who affects others for the worse. Sadly it only needs one rotten apple in the barrel for others to be contaminated at frightening speed.

A negative attitude that is too ingrained to change for the better may undermine all your efforts and possibly place the business itself in jeopardy. It may mean that you have to part company with this person because he or she is a bad influence, no matter how excellent their ability to do the job.

Motivated people have a positive effect on others. When you put a ripe tomato among green tomatoes it will enable them to ripen more rapidly. So it is with people. If there is someone who is positive and enthusiastic, these energies will soon affect the others for the better. If you can use this dynamism to advantage, you will find that maintaining morale is a great deal easier.

Improve surroundings

People tend to work better in pleasant working conditions. Surroundings do not in themselves create motivated people, but they can prevent people from becoming unnecessarily dissatisfied.

Making the workplace more agreeable need not involve a major redesign. It can easily be done. For example:

- Paint the walls from time to time to prevent them from becoming shabby. Newly decorated premises lift people's spirits and give them a fresh start. And if you give them a say in the colour to be painted, this makes people feel involved and raises spirits.
- Choose objects in primary colours, such as red, green and yellow, which keeps people cheerful and makes them smile.

- Provide people with individual coffee mugs which makes them feel wanted.
- Have a decent rest area with relevant trade literature which people would not necessarily buy themselves. This offers them an opportunity to gain further insights into business or professional issues and keeps them abreast of developments.
- Install a soft drinks and/or coffee machine so that people have the freedom to manage their breaks without wasting time.
- Make facilities for food preparation available, especially if you are located off the beaten track. This eliminates the inconvenience of going out for sandwiches or having to make the effort to bring individual provisions to work.
- Improve existing lighting. This is an improvement that can have a dramatic effect on the atmosphere. It can be a positive means of preventing people from becoming tired and irritable.

All these things are positive ways of maintaining performance and letting people know how much they and their efforts are appreciated.

Although there may be some cost involved in providing such facilities and surroundings, the amount of goodwill and the extra effort that is generated usually far outweighs, as well as repays, the additional expense.

Nurture effort

Keeping a high level of motivation requires as much effort on your part as it took to achieving motivation in the first place. It's important to make sure people know what is happening as this inhibits non-productive rumours and enables people to concentrate better on getting their work done.

People need to be clear about how well they are doing their work and accept that corrective action has to be taken when this is required. A periodic overall review allows people to take stock and reminds them how they fit into the bigger picture.

Providing a pleasant environment indicates to people that they are valued and makes the work more congenial. This makes it easier to sustain the effort to produce the required results.

Maintaining morale requires that you stay constantly alert to signs of demotivation. By detecting any changes in levels of enthusiasm, appropriate action can be taken to restore and nurture optimum levels of performance.

Questions to ask yourself

Think about whether you are working positively to sustain people's motivation and answer the following questions:

- Do I keep people informed promptly about things which will affect them?

- Do I take a personal interest in people's work and aspirations?

- Do I help people to rectify their mistakes in a positive way?

- Do I keep a watchful eye on performance and work to redress poor performance promptly?

- Do I help people to review their performance and make action plans for their future development?

- Do I provide the most pleasant surroundings for work that I possibly can?

You will be doing better if…

- You make sure that people get information promptly.

- You take an interest in how well they are performing.

- You identify those areas where performance is not up to standard and take steps to correct it.

- You help them to put together an action plan for their future development.

- You use people's enthusiasm to maintain morale.

- You make the working environment as pleasant as you can within your financial limits.

- You are always prepared to help people do better.

6 Be an inspiring leader

Your own attitude is as important when motivating people as is theirs, because how people behave will be mirrored to a considerable extent by both your attitude and your subsequent behaviour.

Take a positive outlook

If you allow things to get on top of you, you may become demotivated and unwittingly communicate this to others through your behaviour. This in turn will affect their performance adversely. If you behave in a positive way, this will act as a catalyst to others.

By making the work both challenging and fulfilling, people will be motivated to contribute their best. You can demonstrate your positive outlook when you:

- Are enthusiastic about the work in hand.
- Encourage people in their work.
- Are willing to help out when required.
- Let people know you are committed to achieving the task.
- Listen to what people have to say.

Enthusiasm is an essential personal quality when motivating others and you need to keep reminding yourself to:

- See the good rather than the bad.
- Believe wholeheartedly in the overall aims.
- Communicate your beliefs and values clearly.

If you do not allow setbacks to detract from your determination to achieve objectives and if you refuse to take 'No' for an answer, you will be seen as someone who never gives up. This encourages others to have faith in you and behave in the same way.

Your positive outlook influences other people to follow your example. And the more you can help people to be enthusiastic about doing things, the more highly motivated they will be.

Show interest

If you can let people know that you are interested in what they are doing, it stimulates them to get things done. When asking individuals to do something for you, try to put it in a way which indicates that you understand what motivates them. *'I know you enjoy doing this, and I'd be really pleased if you could get it done by Tuesday.'* This is important if you want to ensure they will work hard instead of just turning up.

To be able to show genuine interest, you need to know:

- The particular ambitions of each individual so that you can delegate the right quality of work.

- The skills people would like to acquire, so that you can offer them the opportunity to develop these.

By asking interested questions you can identify the different things that motivate different people. You will soon realise that what motivates one person will not necessarily motivate someone else. This allows you to offer the right opportunities to the right people.

Behave consistently

Since others take their cue from how you behave, it is important that you ensure that you behave consistently. This enables people to know where they stand with you, and have the confidence to predict how you will react in most circumstances.

Behaving consistently means you need to:

- Be sure enough of your objectives and not make spontaneous decisions which could upset the status quo.
- Count to six before reacting, so that you have a chance to work out a more considered response.
- Stay calm in all circumstances, whatever the provocation, so that people know you are in control.

If your moods are unpredictable, others cannot be sure of the reception they will get and so will tend not to admit their problems.

A consistent level of behaviour reassures people and gives them the confidence to share their concerns and to know that they have your full confidence.

Keep up the good work

You know when you are doing the right things because people respond in a positive way and are more productive in their work.

However, on rare occasions, even though you are doing everything you should, someone does not respond. The important thing to realise is that if you are doing everything you should be doing, the problem probably does not rest with you but rather with that individual.

You should endeavour discreetly to find out what is causing an individual's lack of motivation to see if there is anything you can do to improve the situation. But if the problem is so deep-rooted that nothing you can do would improve the situation, you may either have to live with it or consider getting rid of the cause.

If this should happen, try not to let such an experience affect your attitude, even though it can be natural to dwell more on the casualties rather than the successes. A failure with one person or in one situation should not prevent you from trying again with someone else in similar circumstances, because no one person will behave in exactly the same way as another.

Remind yourself that for every person who does not

respond positively there are many more who will, or at least enough to make all your efforts worthwhile.

Cultivate a positive attitude

When you understand the underlying forces and factors which underpin motivation, it is apparent that there is no magic formula which will instantly create motivated people. It is your attitude and subsequent behaviour which are the keys not only to motivating people in the first place, but to keeping them motivated once you have inspired them to do their best.

It is so important to understand what a powerful influence you are in the whole motivating process. By taking a positive approach to working well with people, you go a long way to transforming yourself into an inspirational leader that others will want to follow.

Questions to ask yourself

Think about your attitudes to motivating and answer the following questions:

- Do I work hard to keep my attitude positive despite everything?

- Am I always willing to help when required?

- Do I strive to see the good rather than the bad?

- Do I let people know that I am always interested in what they are doing and how they are getting on?

- Do I make an effort to be even-tempered and approachable in all circumstances?

- Am I aware of how my behaviour will directly affect others' morale and motivation?

- Am I fully committed to motivating people no matter how demanding this may prove?

You will be doing better if…

- Your attitude to motivating is positive.

- You show a genuine interest in other people's work and help them to do better.

- You keep your equilibrium in all circumstances.

- You know how your behaviour can influence the morale and motivation of others.

- You work to keep a high level of enthusiasm and communicate this appropriately.

- You always look for the positive rather than the negative.

- You never give up motivating people, even if it may not work all the time.

Check your progress

If you are finding that motivating others is proving a little more difficult than you thought, think about whether this is because you could have overlooked the need to take account of one or more of the following aspects:

Understand individual needs

If people do not respond, it may be because you have not fully understood that the basic driving forces merely get people out of bed to come to work. They do not make them work harder. It could be that you are offering the wrong things to motivate them. You may also be underestimating people's abilities and not providing them with the right opportunities to work to their capacity or potential.

Make the job fit

If people complain that their work is mundane or boring, it may be that you need to examine the components of the job to see if improvements can be made. Finding out what they would like to do and consulting as to how they think the work could be done will help you do this. By enabling people to take on more responsibility, and providing them with constructive feedback, they are likely to produce better quality work. In this way you can fully involve them and enhance their motivation.

Inspire people to do better

If you find that performance does not seem to be improving, it may be that you have not fully appreciated your role in encouraging others. You need to find the courage to let people take responsibility and do the work in their own way. Allowing people more control makes them want to work harder. Recognising good work and praising it encourages people to want to do better.

Maintain performance

If you find that people's performance is falling off, it may be that you are not maintaining the momentum. You may not be visible enough or are not communicating directly so that people become unsure of what is happening or what is expected of them. Being available to assist and advise as necessary keeps people focused and ensures they feel involved. Taking some care over working conditions makes the place a pleasant one to work in and indicates that people are valued.

Generate enthusiasm

If people get the impression you are simply not interested, it is hardly surprising if they are not motivated. You may perhaps have to indicate more clearly that you want them to enjoy what they are doing and that you care not only about the quality of work they produce but also about them as individuals.

Reap the benefits

Motivating people means understanding what drives and stimulates people to work well. It is achieved through a combination of understanding their individual needs and creating the opportunities for them to want to work well.

The benefits of working with motivated people are that:

- Work will be done to the right standard and within the designated timescales.
- People will enjoy doing the work and feel that they are valuable to your business.
- People will work hard because they want to do what they are doing and feel that is worthwhile.
- Performance will be monitored by the individuals concerned and so they will require much less supervision.
- Morale will be high, which provides an excellent working atmosphere all round.

Once people are motivated, sustaining their momentum requires constant vigilance, but the effort is well worthwhile. The simple and powerful truth is that highly-motivated people perform well and achieve amazing results.

Glossary

Here are some definitions relating to motivating.

Achievement
> *Excelling in the attainment of a goal by hard work and effort.*

Autonomy
> *Having the freedom and discretion to schedule work and determine the procedures to use when carrying it out.*

Competence
> *The ability to do the job.*

Driving forces
> *The basic personal needs that get people out of bed, but do not necessarily motivate them to work better.*

Frustration
> *The difference between expectation and achievement.*

Feedback
> *Assessment of performance which, if communicated correctly, increases performance.*

Hierarchy of needs
> *A pecking order of needs. The satisfaction of lower level ones brings to the fore the higher level ones that still require to be satisfied.*

Incentive
> *Enough enticement to incite action. Make sure it is relevant to the needs of the person involved.*

Job satisfaction

A thorough fulfilment from work.

Morale

A confident attitude of mind demonstrated by positive behaviour and an optimistic outlook.

Motivation

The willingness to exert high levels of effort towards achieving a goal, provided the effort made also satisfies some valued individual need.

Need

The difference between a desired state and the actual state.

Objectives

Direction for effort.

Performance

Dramatic production.

Praise

Warm approbation which encourages people to carry on the good work; a much under-used motivating activity

Responsibility

Being given the power to make decisions and take control.

Reward

Award for all the effort.

Some theories of motivation

A number of theories relating to motivation are regularly mentioned. Here are some of the better known ones.

Maslow's hierarchy of needs theory
Individuals have a hierarchy of five needs – a need for survival, for security, for social intercourse, for self esteem, and for fulfilment of potential. As each need is satisfied, the higher one then becomes more dominant.

Alderfer's ERG theory
According to this theory there are three core needs: existence, relatedness and growth.

Herzberg's motivation-hygiene theory
Intrinsic factors, such as responsibility, recognition and achievement, contribute positively to job satisfaction. Extrinsic factors, such as pay and working conditions, are associated with removing dissatisfaction, but tend not to generate motivation.

McClelland's theory of needs
Achievement, power and affiliation are the three major needs required to create motivation.

Vroom's expectancy theory
Acting in a certain way depends upon the strength of the expectation that the act will be followed by a given outcome, always provided the outcome is attractive enough to warrant the effort.

Further reading

Motivate provides you with an overview of the basic skills you need to develop to help you provide the right context in which you can motivate others.

Below are some other resources which you might find useful when developing and enhancing your skills further in the area of motivating people.

John Adair (2009)
> **Leadership and Motivation:** *The Fifty-Fifty Rule and the Eight Key Principles of Motivating Others* (The John Adair Leadership Library), London: Kogan Page.

Gillian Burn (2008)
> **Motivation for Dummies** (UK Edition), Chichester: John Wiley & Sons Ltd.

Abraham H. Maslow (2013)
> **A Theory of Human Motivation**, Radford, VA: Wilder Publications.

Daniel H Pink (2009)
> **Drive:** *The Surprising Truth About What Motivates Us*, New York, NY: Riverhead Books.

About the author

Kate Keenan, CPsychol, AFBPsS, BA, BSc, MSc, MPhil, has over 20 years experience as a chartered psychologist and is expert in the areas of occupational and organisational psychology. Kate specialises in promoting psychological wellbeing in the workplace. She has worked extensively with corporate and independent businesses, devising strategic management programmes that enable them to identify and resolve managerial issues – from personnel selection and individual assessment to team building and attitude surveys.

She also works as a mentor and coach, offering a series of practical and transformative evidence-based strategies designed to help people make the most of their opportunities, both business and personal. In particular, she helps entrepreneurs and business owners maximise their prime asset – themselves.

Kate has a post-graduate qualification in Mental Health Studies from Kings College, London and currently lives in Bath.

In terms of being able to **motivate** others, she says:

'The secret to motivating lies in providing the right conditions for people to want to succeed. There is always the question of who motivates the motivator. I find it quite an effort to remain motivated, but I am bolstered by the fact that others do not seem to suspect any such effort is required.'

Pocket Manager Books

'Especially for people who neither have the time nor the inclination for ploughing through the normal tomes...'

The Daily Telegraph

Personal wellbeing

- Manage yourself
- Make time
- Assert yourself
- Handle stress

Essential business skills

- Plan
- Solve problems
- Communicate
- Negotiate
- Run meetings

Effective leadership

- Manage
- Recruit
- Motivate
- Delegate
- Understand people

More information about these books available at…

www.kate-keenan.com

To download your FREE Workbook
which accompanies **Motivate**

please visit:

**www.pocketmanagerbooks.com/books/
motivate**

9781909179530

PEFC Certified

This product is
from sustainably
managed forests
and controlled
sources

www.pefc.org

PEFC
PEFC/16-33-415

FSC
www.fsc.org

MIX

Paper from
responsible sourc

FSC® C0049